Merry Christmas
Judy!
May this book bring
you encouragement
on your path.
Love
Kathy
Dec 2017

WISDOM *of* GAIA

Guidance & Affirmations
from the Earth Mother

TONI CARMINE SALERNO

BLUE ANGEL®
PUBLISHING

Wisdom of Gaia

Published by Blue Angel Publishing
80 Glen Tower Drive, Glen Waverley,
Victoria, Australia 3150
E-mail: info@blueangelonline.com
Website: www.blueangelonline.com

Text and Artwork by Toni Carmine Salerno
Edited by Tanya Graham

Blue Angel is a registered trademark of Blue Angel Gallery Pty. Ltd.

ISBN: 978-1-922161-30-7

*Dedicated to Gaia – goddess of the Earth,
my muse and inspiration.
It is through her love, grace and wisdom
that my work comes into existence.*

Introduction

Gaia also spelt Gaea – from Greek;
the Goddess of the Earth'

*

Far back in time, light from the underlying fabric of creation burst forth creating the super-luminous event through which our universe was born. This is when time began, setting forth on an endless journey through ever-expanding space. The early universe was simply a sea of particles floating through space and time. But life's invisible wheels were already in motion and over time, the sea of particles became a sea of stars from which Gaia, our Earth, was born; a living, breathing entity, our Goddess, our Mother and our reflection. 'Gaia', our beautiful planet, is not separate from us and we are not separate from her, just as we are not separate from the Sun, stars and planets that surround us.

We travel through the endless corridors of our mind until one day we find a pathway that leads us to our heart.

The purpose of this book is to point you in love's direction.

She offers guidance, healing and peace. May Gaia be your sanctuary, may she inspire you and may you feel her love. Yet remember that her love and guidance is not confined to the images and words in this book. Gaia's soulful presence can be felt in many ways and her wisdom comes in many forms – for example, through the first words you read when you open a book at random, or a message on a billboard or street sign. Her guidance can even take the form of a perceived setback which steers your life in a whole new direction. It can be a chance encounter, an act of kindness from a stranger or the words of a song. Her guidance is all around us and she presents us with endless possibilities that we can access intuitively by keeping an open heart and mind. Above all, remember that Gaia always guides us to our own heart. For it is through the heart that the ultimate prophecy is revealed – and essentially that prophecy is love.

I sincerely hope you find something in this book that inspires you and helps you to create the life of your dreams.

With love and light,
Toni Carmine Salerno

Tree of Life

*

I am the master of my own destiny.

All I truly desire, I create.

All I create, I create through love.

All I create is for the higher good of all.

I am truly blessed and grateful
for all the abundance in my life.

Moonlight Goddess

*

I give thanks for the healing
that is taking place now in my life.

I express all I feel honestly and lovingly,
without fear or apprehension.

I am safe – I am loved.

I am one with the Goddess.

I am one with the Earth and all creation.

Harmony

*

I am one with the forces of nature.

I am one with the Earth and all creation.

I use my power wisely and to great effect.

I create harmony in my life through love and acceptance.

I achieve my goals with ease.

The Dream

*

I surrender my concerns and fears.

All is revealed at the most perfect moment.

All is well in my life.

I choose trust over doubt.

I remember my dreams and intuitively know
their symbolic language.

Gaia

*

I am in communion with Mother Earth.

I hear her call.

I am grateful for her love
and share her wisdom with others.

I am a beacon of light.

All evolves and unfolds through love.

The Search

*

All is well in my life.

I give thanks for the changing seasons.

In solitude I grow stronger and wiser.

My mind is clear – My heart is open.

I am always on the right path.

Goddess of Creation

*

I take time each day to relax.

I make time each day to nurture my spirit.

I connect spiritually to a space of love inside my heart.

I find peace within.

I am light – I am love.

Attachment

*

I am free from all negative attachment.

I am guided by the power of love.

I look beyond my fears and see only love.

I deserve to be happy.

I choose to follow my heart.

A Hidden Gift

*

I trust that all is unfolding for my highest good.

Love and light fill my heart.

I give thanks for the blessings I receive.

Every ending marks a new beginning.

All lives eternally in my heart.

Jewel Within A Teardrop

*

I am one with my higher self.

I am in touch
and in tune with my innermost feelings.

I am blessed.

I am spiritually connected to those I love.

I am loved.

Rising Above

*

I surrender this situation to the universal power of love.

I trust that all is well in my life.

I look at my life from a higher perspective.

I am divinely guided.

All is clear in my life – I am safe.

Sacred Heart

*

I am in tune with my inner light and wisdom.

I am guided always by love.

I energetically share my light and wisdom with others.

I am one with the Earth and stars.

The guidance I receive is free from the limitations
of time and space.

Reflection

*

My heart is full of love and light.

All is well in my world.

I feel the peace within me
and this creates peace around me.

I observe all I think and feel.

Each negative thought or feeling
is automatically transformed
to love.

Purification (Fire)

*

I listen to my heart and follow its guidance.

I deserve to be happy.

I have the power to create my reality.

I trust that all will work out well.

My life is clear of obstacles.

The Temptress

*

I listen to and trust my intuition.

I look at every situation
from a grounded and balanced point of view.

Every positive has a negative
and vice versa.

I look beyond the superficial
and find the truth.

I look for substance
and I am not swayed by wild promises.

Winter's End

*

I give thanks for the blessings that I receive each day.

All is possible for me now.

All doors are open.

I invite prosperity into my life.

I embrace new opportunities.

Achievement

*

I give thanks
for all the success coming my way.

All I do is a co-creation
with my higher self
and the universal light of love.

I keep focused on my dream.

What I imagine, I create.

I am grateful
for what I have achieved.

Apprehension

*

I surrender my fear and replace it with love.

I surrender my doubt and replace it with confidence.

I see myself moving out into the world with ease.

I give thanks for all I learn and experience.

Each new day is full of possibility.

Eternal Dance

*

I accept change and embrace the new possibilities it brings.

I am flexible and open to new ideas.

I create pleasure in my life.

I look at life from a balanced perspective.

I celebrate life and dance my way through it.

Loss

*

Nothing is missing,
things simply change form.

My life is forever transforming
to ever greater love.

The Earth and I are one.

I am forever protected
and guided by love.

Spiritually,
there is neither beginning nor end.

Remembrance

*

I bless my past and I'm grateful for every experience,
for every experience has helped me
expand my understanding of love.

My life is forever unfolding as it should.

The past, the present and the future are one.

I honour and respect my feelings and emotions,
for they are part of my story.

Sacred Journey

*

The role I play in this life is transient.

I am in essence a being of light.

My family members are some of my greatest teachers.

All human drama helps me expand my awareness of love.

My soul is not confined by time and space.

Night Wind

*

I share my fears and concerns with those I trust and love.

There is nothing to fear, there is only love.

All will soon be resolved.

I am safe – I am loved.

I face my fear and feel it dissolve in a pool of love.

Eternal Love

*

I am physically and emotionally connected
to the healing power
of Mother Earth.

I surround myself with her beauty
and feel a deep sense of peace.

I am free of worry.

Each day I grow stronger
and more relaxed.

My life is in perfect balance.

Liberation

*

I release myself from all negative attachment.

I trust that this is for my highest good.

I trust that this is for the highest good of all.

I help others most.

by not allowing myself or them be co-dependent.

I look at every situation in a balanced way.

Peace

*

I trust in the power of love.

I trust that all will unfold as it should.

My mind is like a clear blue sky.

My heart is filled with love.

All upon this Earth is bathed in a sea of love.

Enchanted Forest

*

I am open to new ideas and adventures.

Life is full of endless creative possibility.

I embrace each opportunity that comes my way.

I love the magic and mystery of life.

I trust my heart – I believe in love.

The Message

*

I thank the Earth and stars for every blessing.

I give thanks for the love that fills and surrounds me.

I am loved unconditionally by a benevolent universe.

My mind is full of light.

My heart is forever grateful.

Thinking of You

*

All I love lives forever in my heart.

I am one with all humanity.

I am one with all creation.

I am in constant communion with everyone.

Time and space are real only when I believe they are.

Flame Tree

*

A creative flame glows within my heart
and illuminates my mind.

I am ready to start something new.

My heart and mind are open to new possibilities.

My dream becomes my reality.

I do what I love and love what I do.

Ganesha

*

I am protected and guided by a higher power.

When the path is blocked, I take this as a sign to wait.

I give thanks for divine intervention.

When the path is clear, I move forward with ease.

All that occurs or does not occur is for my highest good.

Purification (Water)

*

I allow all unresolved feelings to surface.

I give thanks for the healing that is taking place.

I am emotionally cleansed.

I am free of emotional baggage.

I release all that no longer serves me.

Healing

*

My sanctuary is a space of light inside my heart.

I find peace and contentment within.

My heart reveals my truth.

My heart reflects the real me.

My heart guides me.

Hidden Path

*

My heart and mind
are in perfect alignment.

My heart's desire
and my thoughts are one.

I am a spiritual being
in a physical body.

The journey ahead
is filled with light.

The light of my soul
illuminates my path.

Lost Love

*

All I experience in life has a purpose and is meaningful.

Everything is part of a higher plan.

Every experience expands my understanding
and appreciation of love.

The truth is what is.

The truth is what was.

The truth is what will be.

Moonlight

*

I invite romance into my life.

I look at things from a new perspective.

My life is full of unlimited potential.

Creative possibilities are all around me.

Life is an endless source of inspiration.

Nine of Hearts

*

I am blessed.

I am protected.

I am grateful.

I am fulfilled.

I am love.

Zen Garden

*

I accept and love the world as it is.

I trust that there is a higher order to everything.

I find solace in the sanctuary of my heart.

I move my awareness within.

I am the peace I seek.

Perception

*

I honour another's truth but stand firm within my own.

I am comfortable with who I am.

I keep an open heart and mind.

I empower myself when I honour my values.

In being true to me I am also true to others.

Yin Yang

*

I love and accept all that I am.

There is nothing to change,
there is only love.

Every aspect of me
serves both me and others in some way.

I create health, wealth and harmony
by loving what is.

All I accept and love
transforms to ever greater love.

Amethyst

*

I give thanks for the transformation
and healing that has taken place.

I move through life with gratitude.

I move through life with certainty.

I move through life with confidence.

I achieve my goals.

What I focus on, I create.

Sacred Earth Mother

*

I am in essence light.

I am in essence soul.

I am pure creative potential.

I am guided by my heart.

I apply love and wisdom to all I say and do.

Intuitive Communication

*

I focus on my inner world.

I am one with all creation.

All is energetically connected.

I trust my intuition.

My awareness expands through love.

Ocean of Eternal Love

*

Love heals.

Love brings resolution.

Love conquers.

Love creates.

Love is eternal.

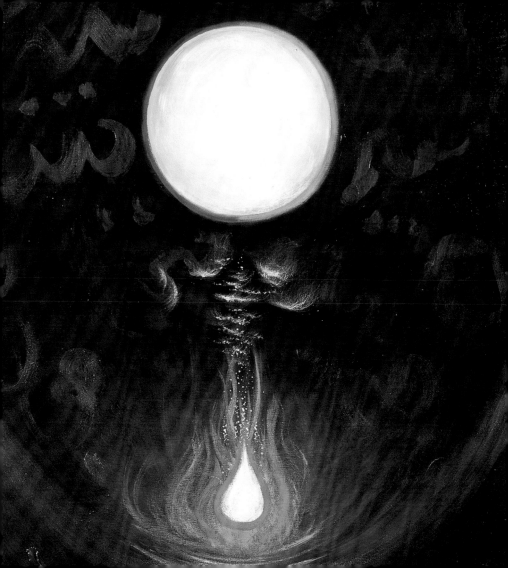

Evolution

*

All lovingly unfolds through time and space.

Life constantly transforms, but in essence nothing changes.

There is nothing to fear, there is only love.

I am one with the universe and stars.

Love is my guiding force.

About the Artist & Author

Toni Carmine Salerno is the author of numerous books, CDs and oracle cards. He is also an artist who paints intuitively; depicting themes associated with mind, body and spirit. Born in Melbourne, Australia to Italian parents, the work of this internationally acclaimed self-taught artist and author and his publishing house Blue Angel Publishing is having a significant and positive effect on people's lives around the globe, connecting people and cultures through the unifying force of love and helping to break down the barriers of out-moded ways of thinking. Toni and everyone at Blue Angel hope to inspire all through the power of unconditional love.

You can find out more about Toni Carmine Salerno by visiting his website: **www.tonicarminesalerno.com**

For more information on this
or any Blue Angel Publishing release,
please visit our website at:

www.blueangelonline.com